STRINGS

AN INTRODUCTION TO MUSICAL INSTRUMENTS

By Dee Lillegard

CHILDRENS PRESS ®

CHICAGO

PHOTO CREDITS

© Cameramann International, Ltd.—8, 12, 19, 24, 28

Journalism Services:

© Rick Bamman—15, 20
© Dave Brown—7
© Paul F. Gero—21 (top)
© Joseph Jacobson—4
© Mike Kidulich—26
© John Patsch—22 (bottom)
© Charles Schabes—9, 27

© Mary Messenger—11, 14

© Norma Morrison—6

Nawrocki Stock Photo:

© David Bentley—3, 21 (bottom)
© Michael Brohm—13
© Robert Lightfoot—5, 10, 17, 29
© Christina Mackenzie—25
© Carlos Vergara—18
© Charles Yapp—22 (top)

© Karen Yops—23

Art: Tom Dunnington—30, 31

Library of Congress Cataloging-in-Publication Data

Lillegard, Dee.
    Strings / by Dee Lillegard.
        p.   cm. — (An introduction to musical
instruments)
    Summary: A brief introduction to the musical
instruments of the strings family.
    ISBN 0-516-02219-9
    1. Stringed instruments—Juvenile
literature. [1. Stringed instruments.] I. Title.
II. Series: Lillegard, Dee. Introduction to musical
instruments.
ML460.L53   1988   87-32994
787—dc19   CIP
                                        AC MN

Childrens Press®, Chicago

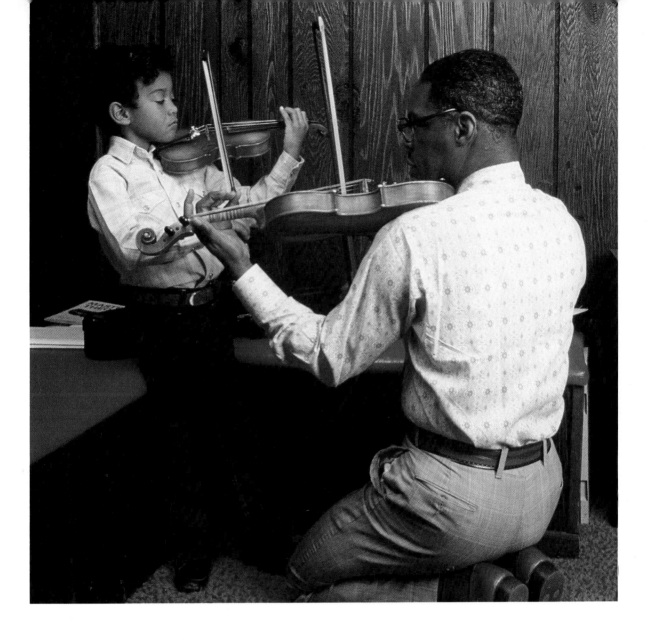

Hey, diddle diddle,
The cat and the fiddle ...
Do you know this old
rhyme? Do you know what
a fiddle is?

The violin has four strings. Each string makes a different sound.

A fiddle is a **violin**.
It is a **string instrument**!
Let's join the cat and play
some strings.

4

There are four members of the **violin** family. Every member of this family looks the same. But each one is a different size.

Violin

Viola

Cello

Bass

To play the **violin**, you
will need a bow. The bow is
like a magic wand. It makes
music come out of the **violin's**
empty box, or *belly*.

The bow is made of wood
and hair from the tails of
white horses. You must never
touch the hairs on the bow.
The oil from your fingers can
ruin them.

Hold the **violin** to your chin. Run the bow across the strings. *Screech! Screech!* Don't feel bad. The **violin** is not easy to play.

But if you practice, you can

make beautiful bright sounds
and soft, sweet sounds on the
violin. You can make ghostly
sounds, too! You can even
pluck the strings with your
fingers, if you want.

*The violin and viola are played in symphony
orchestras.*

The **viola** is a little
bigger than the **violin**. It
makes a lower, more mellow
sound. But it is played
just like the **violin**.

You hold the **viola** under
your chin, too. Take the bow
in one hand and use the
fingers of your other hand to
hold down the strings. This
makes different notes.

An end pin holds the cello off the ground.

The **cello** is much bigger than a **violin** or a **viola**. You can't put a **cello** under your chin. It stands on the floor, and you hold it between your knees.

The **cello** makes a warm
and very mellow sound. Its
tones are lower and deeper
than the **viola's**.

All the instruments in
the **violin** family are
played in a symphony
orchestra.

The **double bass** is the
giant of the **violin** family.
Its tones are even lower than
the **cello's**. It sounds a
little like a bullfrog. What
a deep voice!

The harp is one of the oldest known stringed instruments. It has forty-seven strings and seven foot-pedals.

The **harp** is another string instrument. You do not need a bow to play the **harp**. You pluck it with your fingers. It makes a heavenly sound.

The **guitar** belongs to
another family of strings.
Guitars are not played with a
bow. You use your fingers to
strum or pluck its strings.
You can also use a pick.

People played the guitar in Egypt 5,000 years ago.
Most guitars have six strings. Some have four and
others have twelve.

Some people play the
guitar and sing. Spanish
people dance the exciting
flamenco to **guitar** music. If
you play the **guitar**, you
could be in a band.

Use a small piece of
tortoiseshell to pluck the
strings of the **mandolin**.
People sing and dance to

*Indians dressed in their native costume play
mandolins during a Mexican celebration.*

mandolin music. Sometimes
a **mandolin** is played in
an orchestra.

The **banjo** is an American
instrument that came from
Africa. **Banjos** are fun to play.

The **ukulele** is a small instrument. It's not very hard to play. People in Hawaii sing and dance to the sound of the **ukulele**.

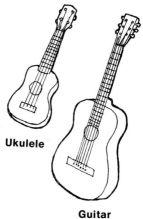

Ukulele

Guitar

Play a **string** instrument.
Use a bow, a pick, or just
your fingers.
Strings can be fun!

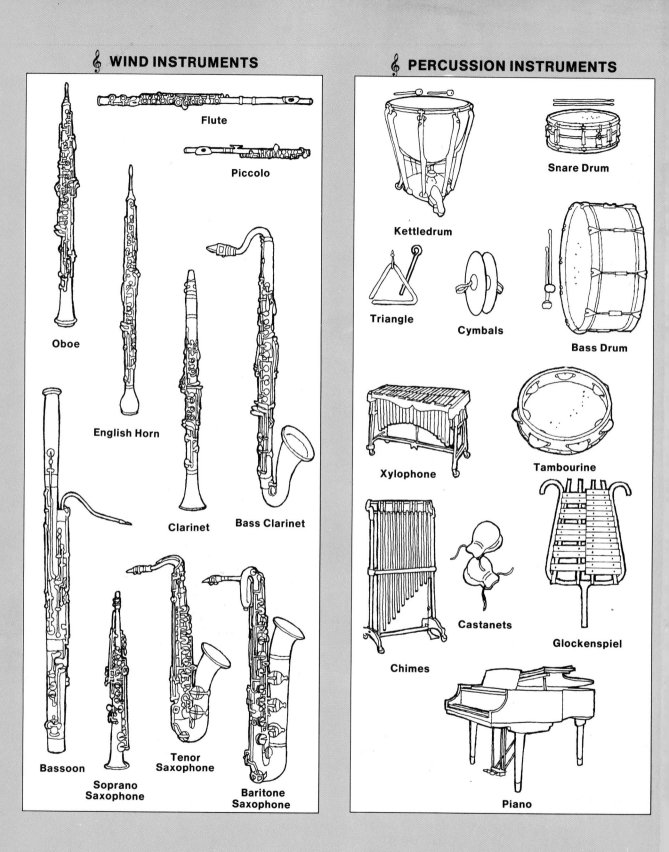

♪ WIND INSTRUMENTS

Flute

Piccolo

Oboe

English Horn

Clarinet

Bass Clarinet

Bassoon

Soprano Saxophone

Tenor Saxophone

Baritone Saxophone

♪ PERCUSSION INSTRUMENTS

Kettledrum

Snare Drum

Triangle

Cymbals

Bass Drum

Xylophone

Tambourine

Chimes

Castanets

Glockenspiel

Piano

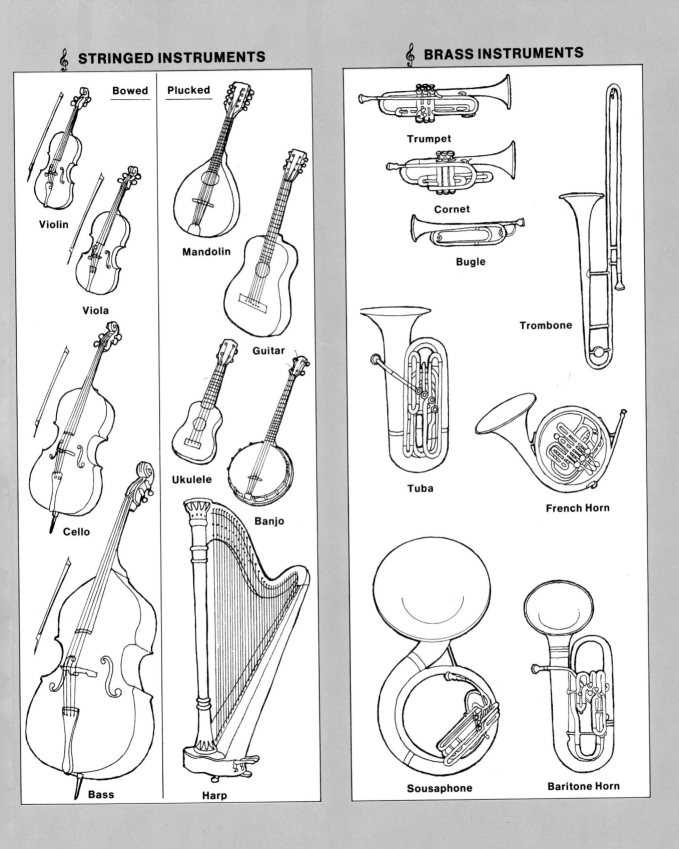

STRINGED INSTRUMENTS

Bowed | Plucked

Violin

Viola

Cello

Bass

Mandolin

Guitar

Ukulele

Banjo

Harp

BRASS INSTRUMENTS

Trumpet

Cornet

Bugle

Trombone

Tuba

French Horn

Sousaphone

Baritone Horn

ABOUT THE AUTHOR

Dee Lillegard (born Deanna Quintel) is the author of over two hundred published stories, poems, and puzzles for children, plus *Word Skills*, a series of high-interest grammar worktests, and *September to September*, *Poems for All Year Round*, a teacher resource. Ms. Lillegard has also worked as a children's book editor and teaches writing for children in the San Francisco Bay area. She is a native Californian.